SNOWY OWL
Ulchabhán Sneachtúil

Gabriel Rosenstock

© Gabriel Rosenstock 2025
Layout by Mandy Marcus

SNOWY OWL
Ulchabhán Sneachtúil

Bilingual haiku for older children with a stunning gallery of international art including eye-popping street art, spooky US government posters and stirring photographs of US child labour.

"Sneeuwuil" (1927)
Samuel Jessurun de Mesquita (1868–1944)

Preface

Artwork used in this book of haiku and senryū for older children falls under Public Domain or Fair Use, i.e. artwork that is widely available on the internet, on such platforms as Artvee, Wikicommons and Wikiart.

~

Senryū look like haiku but are intended as playful squibs. Indeed, haiku were essentially playful compositions until great depth and resonance were added to them by such Japanese grandmasters as Bashō, Chiyo-ni, Issa, Buson, Shiki and Santōka. Later, in the 20th century, haiku masters and haiku organisations came to the fore in dozens of countries throughout the world.

~

It's best to **dip** into haiku books, such as this one, rather than read them from cover to cover. In fact, haiku is an awakening experience so if you stop reading and then read the same haiku a week later, you might experience something else entirely! So, were you asleep a week ago, or are you asleep now?!

~

Texts in *Snowy Owl* range from the lyrical to the contemplative, the questioning to the absurd, and are suitable for readers 10–13+.

Gabriel Rosenstock

Amstardam
cara á lorg
ag neach éigin

Amsterdam
a creature is looking
for a friend

Lewis Hine (SAM / *USA*)

ciseáin! ciseáin!
cé a cheannóidh
ár gcuid ciseán?

baskets! baskets!
who will buy
our baskets?

Ernst Stückelberg (An Eilvéis / *Switzerland*)

hmm . . . cé thusa? arsa an cailín
cé thusa?
a d'fhreagair an laghairt

      hmm . . . and you are? *asked the girl*
      and you are?
      answered the lizard

Edward Julius Detmold (An Bhreatain / *Britain*)

an chiaróg bheannaithe
cá mbeimis
dá huireasa?

> *the sacred beetle*
> *where would we be*
> *without it?*

Ernst Schiess (An Eilvéis / *Switzerland*)

aoire dhá chaora . . .
ní raibh sé in ann
idirdhealú eatarthu

there once was a shepherd
with only two sheep . . .
he forgot which was which

Lewis Hine (SAM / *USA*)

brostaígí!
tá na milliúnaithe ag feitheamh . . .
monarcha todóg

hurry up lads!
the millionaires are waiting . . .
cigar factory

Pierre-Auguste Renoir (An Fhrainc / *France*)

ag éisteacht
le tae á dhoirteadh
cluas cupáin

listening
to tea being poured
ear of a cup

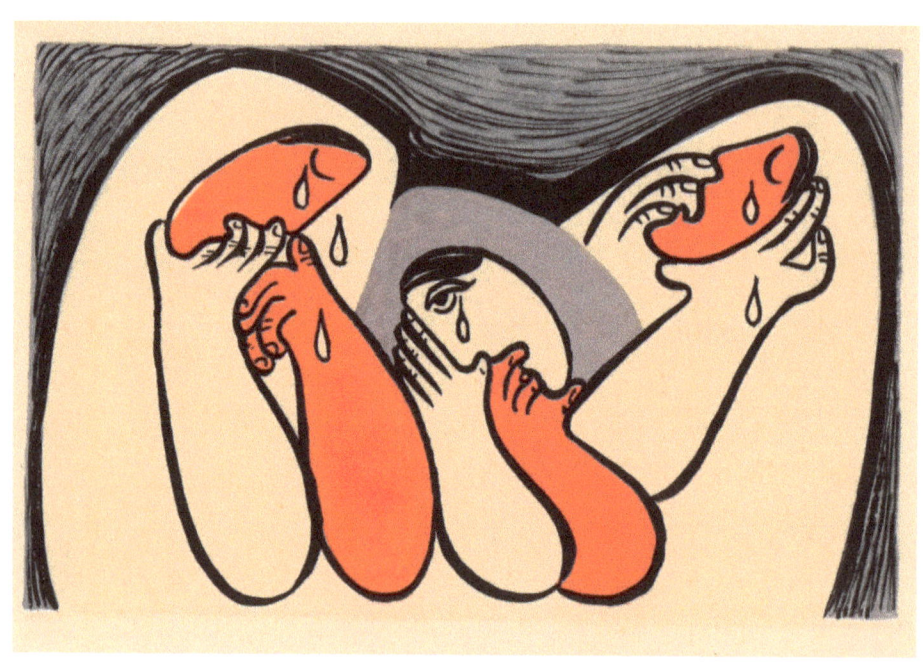

Mikuláš Galanda (An tSlóvaic / *Slovakia*)

na Cumhachtaí Móra
cuirid mná ag gol –
nach mór atáid!

the Great Powers*
they cause women to weep –
how great they are!

*China, France, Russia, the United Kingdom, and the United States are referred to as the Great Powers. The Great Powers have been complicit in wars, conflicts and arms deals worth billions and there will never be a fair and just world, a peaceful world, as long they are up to their shenanigans!

Lewis Hine (SAM / *USA*)

haigh, mise Norma
aois: a deich
piocaimse 100 punt cadáis sa lá

hi, I'm Norma, aged 10
my target? a hundred pounds of cotton
a day

Cornelis Biltius (An Ísliltír / *Netherlands*)

ar a shlí abhaile a bhí sé
nuair a lámhachadh é
creabhar

> *shot*
> *on his way home*
> *woodcock*

UP WITH ENGLISH

Supplementary English Teaching Materials (EFL) Available From The U.S. Information Service (USIS)

AMERICAN CIVILIZATION
AMERICAN IDIOMS
ENGLISH FOR SPECIFIC PURPOSES (ESP)

GRAMMAR
INTEGRATED SKILLS
LANGUAGE ACTIVITIES

LISTENING SKILLS
ORAL SKILLS
READING SKILLS

TEACHER TRAINING RESOURCES
WRITING SKILLS

**FOR MORE INFORMATION:
CONTACT YOUR NEAREST USIS OFFICE.**

US Information Agency

an Nachuáitlis go deo
an Haváis go deo
an Navachóis go deo

up with Nahuatl
up with Hawaiian
up with Navajo

Lewis Hine (SAM / *USA*)

scileadh oisrí
sea, a chara . . .
obair mhaslach

shucking oysters
yes, my friend . . .
it sucks

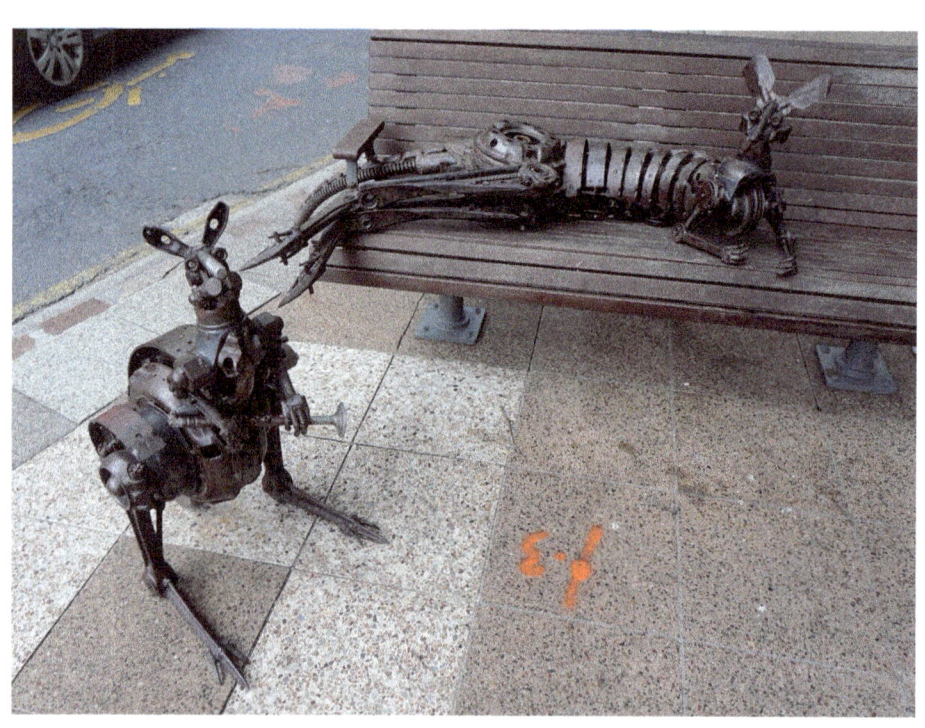

(An Astráil / *Australia*)

scíth á glacadh acu
cangarúnna
an lae amárach

taking a rest
kangaroos
of the future

Leopold Kupelwieser (An Ostair / *Austria*)

stánadh folamh
a chuid línte dearmadta
ag aisteoir

blank stare
an actor forgets
his lines

Hermann Kern (An Ostair / *Austria*)

gabha stáin
ag casúireacht . . .
glór an phiasúin

*hammering
of a tinsmith . . .
cackling pheasant*

Lewis Hine (SAM / *USA*)

féachann sé níos sine
ná mar atá sé
piocadóir caor

looking older
than his years
berry picker

John Gould (An Bhreatain / *Britain*)

pé slí
a bhféachann tú air
is domhan bunoscionn é

whichever way
you look at it
it's an upside down world

Roelant Savery (Flóndras / *Flanders*)

slán
slán leis an saol aoibhinn seo!
an dódó deireanach ar domhan

goodbye
sweet world, goodbye!
last dodo on earth

Alfred Guillou (An Fhrainc / *France*)

obair mhall
obair dhian
diúilicíní a bhailiú

slow work
hard work
gathering mussels

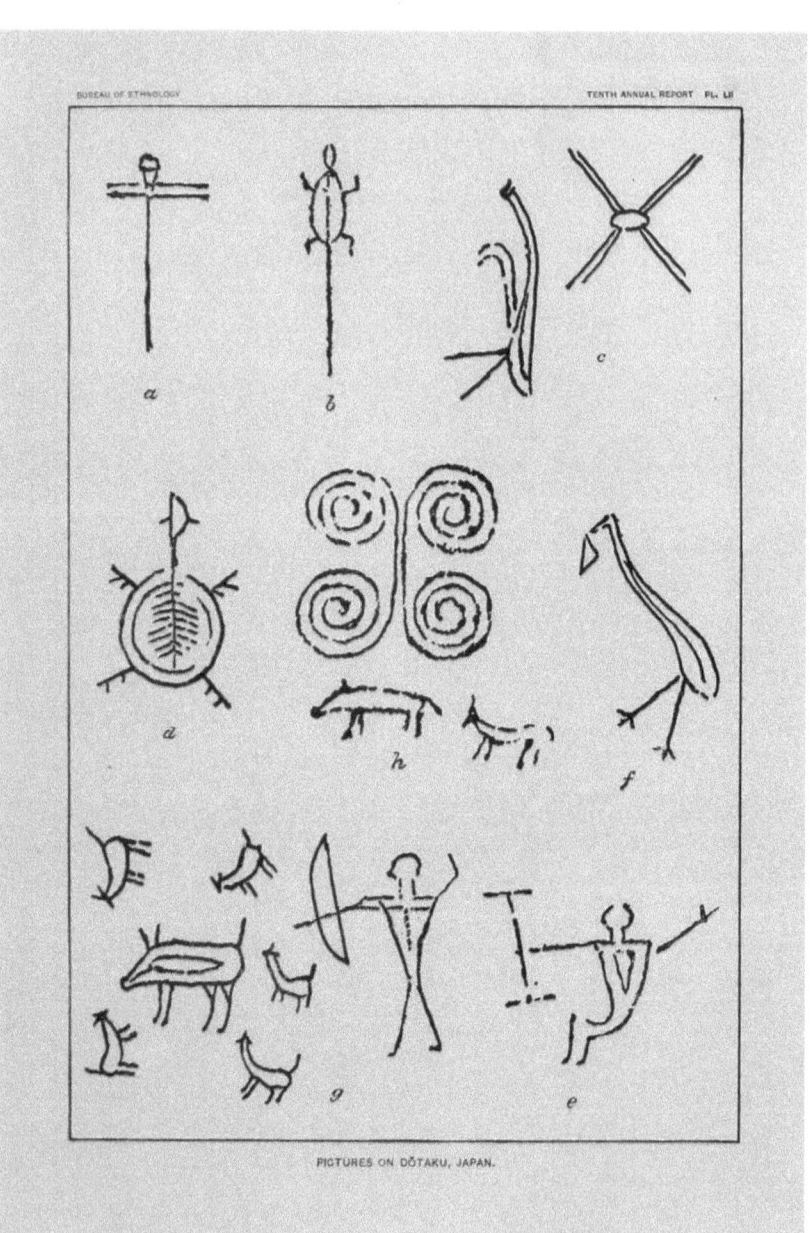

Garrick Mallery (SAM / *USA*)

scriobláil
an bhfuil ciall ar bith
le scriobláil an tsaoil seo?

squiggles
of this world
what do they mean?

Lewis Hine (SAM / *USA*)

Merilda
is ainm dom
iompróir mónóg

my name is Merilda*
I carry
cranberries

*Merilda is a variant of Muriel, from the Irish 'muir gheal', meaning 'bright sea'.

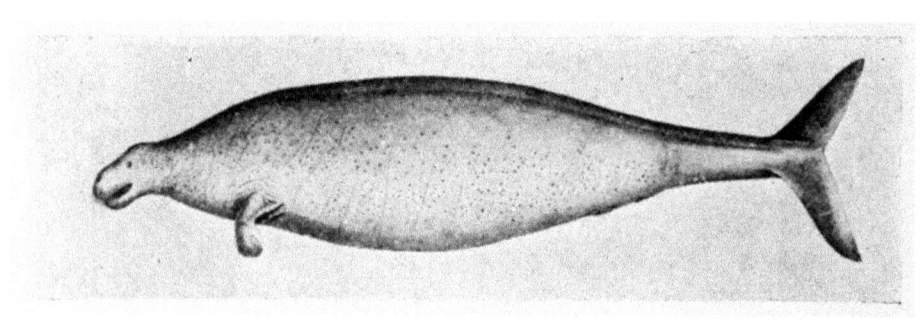

Georg Wilhelm Steller (An Ghearmáin / *Germany*)

imithe
ní thiocfaidh sí ar ais go deo
bó mhara

    gone! gone
    she's not coming back
    sea-cow

Georg Forster (An Ghearmáin / *Germany*)

cait a stoll í
an phearaicít uchtdubh
dheireanach

she met her doom
savaged by cats
black-fronted parakeet

François-Nicolas Martinet (An Fhrainc / *France*)

ba bhlasta é
agus é ramhar deirtear
druid húpú

fat ones were tasty
or so they say
hoopoe starling

Canis antarcticus

Beagle Voyage

ní raibh aon ghrá
idir é agus na Briotanaigh
faolchú na Malvinas

*no love lost
between them: the British
and Falkland Islands wolves*

Aloys Zötl (An Ostair / *Austria*)

bhíodh leathchéad acu
i dtréad: bailithe leo anois atáid –
quagga

they'd roam
in herds of fifty
now they've vanished – quagga

Lewis Hine (SAM / *USA*)

pónairí a scileadh?
sea, go deimhin
is mór an spórt é!

stringing beans?
oh, yeah–honestly
it's great fun!

Mstislav Dobuzhinsky (An Rúis – An Liotuáin / *Russia – Lithuania*)

AR IARRAIDH
dán de chuid
Constantin Sunnerberg

MISSING
a poem by
Constantin Sunnerberg

Jean-Baptiste Paul Lazerges (An Fhrainc / *France*)

'bhfuil eolas acu ar réaltaí
is ar réaltbhuíonta?
camaill

    can they read the stars
    and constellations?
    camels

Lewis Hine (SAM / *USA*)

haigh, mise Glenn . . .
aois? a haon déag
(braithim go bhfuilim céad bliain
d'aois)

>*hi there, I'm Glenn . . .*
>*age? eleven*
>*(I feel like I'm a hundred)*

Gustav Wentzel (An Iorua / *Norway*)

níl sé éasca
bheith díomhaoin . . .
feirmeoir ar scor

not easy
doing nothing . . .
retired farmer

(An Bhealarúis / *Belarus*)

"cé? Kuzma Chorny?
níor chuala trácht air!"
arsa an leabharlannaí

"who? Kuzma Chorny?
nope! never heard of him!"
says the librarian

Eastman Johnson (SAM / *USA*)

pub i mBostún
seanfhear ag canadh faoin gcailín
a fágadh in Éirinn

Boston pub
an old man sings
The Girl I Left Behind Me

Lewis Hine (SAM / *USA*)

8 mbliana d'aois atáim
Jaic is ainm dom
bliteoir

I'm 8
Jack's the name
milking's my game

William Aiken Walker (SAM / *USA*)

saothrú do dhaoine eile?
cén fáth nach saothróimis
le chéile – dá chéile!

why work for others?
can't we all work together –
for each other?

Elihu Vedder (SAM / *USA*)

scáthanna an tráthnóna . . .
cuimhne ar ní
atá ar tí tarlú

    shades of evening . . .
    a memory of something
    that's about to happen

Johannes Gerardus Keulemans (An Ísiltír / *Netherlands*)

hoa . . .
ní raibh seans faoin spéir aige
in aghaidh na bhfrancach

    *hoa . . .
    not a snowball's chance in hell
    against the rats

*(The name on the Hawaiian island of Molokai for the extinct black mamo)

Lewis Hine (SAM / *USA*)

tá's agat cad deirtear
an té nach gcuirfidh greim
cuirfidh sé dhá ghreim

you know what they say
a stitch in time
saves nine

Jules Bastien-Lepage (An Fhrainc / *France*)

Díoiginéas is a lampa
duine cóir fós
á lorg aige

Diogenes with his lamp
still searching
for an honest man

Paul Klee (An Eilvéis & An Ghearmáin / *Switzerland & Germany*)

oscail do chlab–
scaoil amach é! faic!
taibhse an ghairdín

open your mouth–
spit it out! nothing!
garden ghost

Lewis Hine (SAM / *USA*)

raidisí
raidisí
úra!

radishes
fresh
radishes!

Stormie Mills (An Astráil / *Australia*)

níl sé in ann
cur suas leis an ngrian . . .
súmaire

can't stand
the sight of the sun . . .
vampire

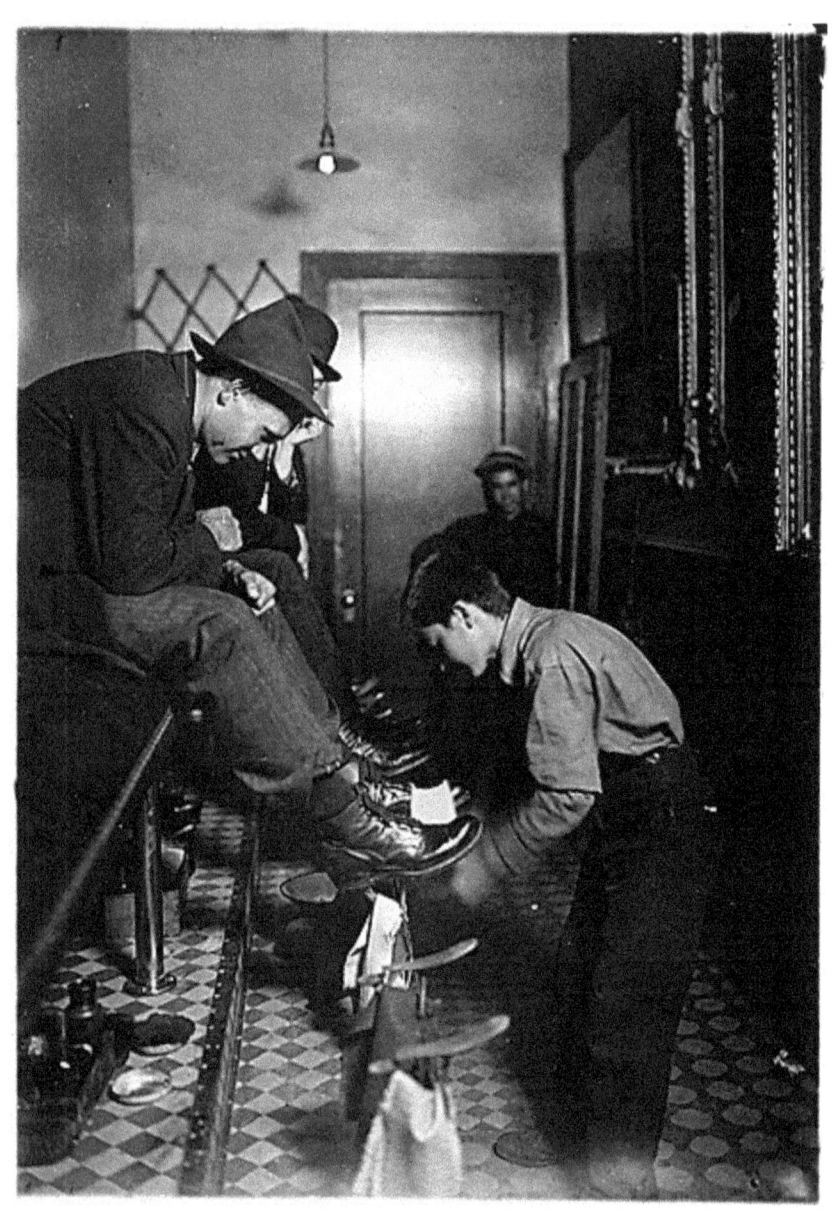

Lewis Hine (SAM / *USA*)

lá
i ndiaidh lae
boladh snasa

day in
day out
smell of polish

Félix Vallotton (An Fhrainc / *France*)

gabhann an phéist
níos doimhne sa chré –
cogadh ar siúl ag daoine arís

*worms go deeper
in the soil –
men at war again!*

Jean Baptiste Paul Lazerges (An Fhrainc / *France*)

bíonn scíth
uathusan leis
Beidiúnaigh

they too
need a rest
Bedouins

Da Loria Norman (SAM / *USA*)

cé a labhraíonn
inniu ina taobh
Fand

    who speaks of her now
    the lady known as
    Fand

Lewis Hine (SAM / *USA*)

síos tollán dorcha leo
aislingí uile
an mhianadóra óig

down a dark tunnel
all the dreams
of a young miner

Gustave Doré (An Fhrainc / *France*)

na Garbhchríocha
agus an teanga tráth
ina sreabha

Scottish Highlands
the Gaelic tongue
as plentiful once as her streams

Carolus-Duran (An Fhrainc / *France*)

Étienne Haro
bhí cáil air tráth as
hmm . . . rud éigin

Étienne Haro
once famous for
hmm . . . something or other

John Bauer (An tSualainn / *Sweden*)

ar fhág tú
babhla bainne amach dó?
an gruagach

> *have you left*
> *his milk out for him?*
> *the broonie*

Lewis Hine (SAM / *USA*)

Henry & Hilda
6 & 3
sách sean chun biatas a phiocadh

Henry & Hilda
6 & 3 years of age
old enough to pick beet

Tadeusz Makowski (An Pholainn / *Poland*)

glanann sé an ceo
den aigne
haiku

*it scatters
mental fog
haiku*

Klemens Brosch (An Ostair / *Austria*)

an mbraitheann siad é
nuair a bhuaileann siad an talamh?
duilleoga

do they feel it
when they hit the ground?
falling leaves

Serhi Svetoslavsky (An Úcráin / *Ukraine*)

cúpla storc
froganna aimsithe acu
de réir dealraimh

a couple of storks
looks like they've found
some frogs

Eduardo Kobra (An Bhrasaíl / *Brazil*)

aoibh uirthi
Anne Frank
aoibh

smiling
Anne Frank
smiling

Maurice & Edmund Detmold (RA / *UK*)

an choir admhaithe ag an ngadaí . . .
ualach trom bainte
dá chroí

the thief confesses . . .
a great burden is lifted
from his heart

Edward Julius Detmold (An Bhreatain / *Britain*)

a croí ag dul amach
go dtí an domhan go léir
maintis chrábhaidh

> *its heart goes out*
> *to the whole world*
> *praying mantis*

Lewis Hine (SAM / *USA*)

léigh ina thaobh!
cosc ar dhúshaothrú
leanaí!

read all about it!
child labour
banned!

Osman Hamdi Bey (An Tuirc / *Turkey*)

'dul chun cinn mall'
a scríobhann sé ina dhialann
traenálaí toirtísí

'progress is slow'
he writes in his diary
tortoise trainer

Lewis Hine (SAM / *USA*)

scoil in Kentucky
fonn ar na cearca féin
rud éigin a phiocadh suas

school in Kentucky
even hens
want to pick up something

Nicholas Roerich (An Rúis / *Russia*)

ag lorg rianta mo chos
sa sneachta atá sé
yeití

out there
searching for my footprints
in the snow . . . yeti

Archibald Thorburn (Albain / *Scotland*)

ookpik! ulchabhán sneachtúil!
cad atá ionat?
labhair!

ookpik! snowy owl!
what are you?
speak!

Iarfhocal / Afterword

Why is this book called *Snowy Owl*? For no other reason than that I very much like the work of Dutch artist Samuel Jessurun de Mesquita.

His wonderful *Orang-Utan* features in another book of haiku for older children, now in published form and originally appearing as a PDF on the free platform freekidsbooks.org

Why did I issue the books *Snowy Owl* and *Orang-Utang* as free books originally? Is an orang-utan dependent on money? Does it think about money? Of course not! Has the orang-utan got a bank account? No, he's not mad! D. H. Lawrence called money 'our great collective madness'. Was he right?

There once lived a man called Shūsui Kōtoku. Guess what he said! 'Abolish money!' That's exactly what he said. What happened to him? They executed him, of course. The orang-utans wouldn't have executed him, nor the snowy owls . . . No, siree Bob!

But, you say, 'Hey, Mr Rosenstock! Your head must be in the clouds. I need money to buy myself a new pair of jeans.' Money is important! Is it?

The Sermon on the Mount has a "found haiku":

> consider the lilies of the field
> they neither toil
> nor spin

Must everything be a financial transaction? Maybe you haven't thought much about money? You see, we don't think a lot about things which we all take for granted. One could say that haiku is a way of waking up from this trance and becoming more aware. What's going on? Benjamin Franklin said:

> *Money has never made man happy, nor will it; there is nothing in its nature to produce happiness. The more of it one has the more one wants.*

Was he right? An American journalist, Sydney J. Harris said:

Men make counterfeit money; in many more cases, money makes counterfeit men.

I wanted the book *Orang-Utan* to be free. I wanted it to be completely free of the whole business of money. That is why I decided to publish *Orang-Utan* under the Creative Commons license and allow it to be freely used by thousands as a PDF. Now you have to pay for it, unfortunately!

WHAT IS A TÖGRÖG?

One way or the other, I feel I don't "own" the haiku in *Orang-Utan*. You can do what you like with them. Translate them into Mongolian? Go ahead! I won't charge you a tögrög. That's what Mongolian currency is called. The word means 'a circle' and *tögrög sar* means 'a full moon!'

The haiku in *Orang-Utan* came to me spontaneously, from out of the blue. How can I call them "mine"?

How many *tögrög* would a consumer need to buy the *tögrög sar*? People have become consumers and their buying patterns are tracked by algorithms. It's a plot!

There's an American TV station and its mantra is

CAPITALISE ON IT! I'm going for a walk. Capitalise on it! I'm going to write an ode to a nightingale. Capitalise on it! Excuse me, I'm going to sneeze. Capitalise on it! What a mantra!

Have you heard of Creative Commons? It's been around for 25 years or so and it has licensed over two and a half billion items in that period – freeing writings, artwork and other creations so that people can share them and enjoy them on platforms such as YouTube, Flickr and Wikipedia!

Do you think Creative Commons is a good idea? I looked at de Mesquita's orang-utan, I looked at his snowy owl, and they said: 'You don't own me, buddy! Don't capitalise on me, please! I want to be free!'

Not all of my books are free. But I might liberate a few more of them!

> *I think the person who takes a job in order to live–that is to say, for the money–has turned himself into a slave.*
> Joseph Campbell

How to free oneself from slavery? Firstly, you must ask yourself are you completely free. Really? Are you free from what George Woodcock called The Tyranny of the Clock?

Are you free of harmful habits, of gadgets such as smartphones, video games and so on? Do you live in a society where some people's freedom is restricted? You could take the Gandhian path, civil disobedience, and protest against laws or conditions which curtail freedom. Freekidsbooks.org has a book about Gandhi for older children. If you feel you are ready for it, download it today: https://freekidsbooks.org/walk-with-gandhi/

Only *you* can say what freedom means to you. Is what Campbell says true? He's implying that we all grow up to become wage slaves! There's more to life than that, surely?

CHILDREN HAVE RIGHTS!

Freedom! Political freedom, cultural freedom, religious freedom– freedom of speech. Why are we talking about such matters here? Are these not adult concerns? No, incorrect. Children have rights as well! Many young people are unaware of their rights.

An Indian platform, StoryWeaver which makes hundreds of free books available for children in many languages, outlines all of your rights as a child: it's called *I Know My Rights* and you can download it free.

Those rights were established and explained by the United Nations Convention on the Rights of the Child. One of your rights is that you are entitled to access knowledge; it is not a privilege for the few–you are entitled to the enjoyment and illumination which the arts provide, including haiku! Got it?

If you think a haiku is a harmless description of butterflies, snails, rain, orang-utans, snow or whatever, don't forget that haiku poets in the 1940s, in Japan, were persecuted for their anti-war views.

I have made countless StoryWeaver free books available in Irish, a threatened language, on the Léigh Leat platform.

Whether I charge for books or give them away for nothing, I'm not writing for money. I'm writing for you! Good idea? Yes. A great philosopher, Arthur Schopenhauer (1788 -1860), explains why:

> *Writing for money and preservation of copyright are, at bottom, the ruin of literature. It is only the man who writes absolutely for the sake of the subject that writes anything worth writing . . . The best works of great men all come from the time when they had to write either for nothing or for very little pay . . .*

In a world which has deified money and commerce, Schopenhauer sounds like he should be locked up!

Giving away a free book asks us all to think of the way the world works. Is there a better way? What do you think?

> *A nation that continues year after year to spend more money on military defence than on programs of social uplift is approaching spiritual doom.*

So said Martin Luther King, Jr.

I hope you thoroughly enjoy most of the artwork in *Snowy*

Owl as well as the incredible photographs taken by Lewis Hine which help us to see how so many children lived and toiled just over a century ago!

> sléacht roimhe, a ghearrchaile
> is dia é an meaisín!
> sléacht roimhe

> *bow down, young girl*
> *the machine is god!*
> *bow down*

A final thought about money. Isn't it a crying shame that the great chronicler of child labour in America, Lewis Hine, died in poverty? What kind of a world was it which sent children out to work, instead of receiving an education and enjoying their hobbies and games? Lewis Hine received death threats for exposing the evil of child labour! What kind of world would allow the person who recorded child labour to die penniless?

    Well, all that is history, you say. It doesn't happen anymore! Would you believe me if I said that in this decade, the 2020s, there are at least 160 million child labourers in the world, in the 5-17 age-group?

Let's look again at de Mesquita's orang-utan:

The animal is quietly minding his own business, grooming himself, and looks friendlier than a lot of people I know. Orang-utan is a Malay word: *orang* means 'a person' and *hutan* means 'a forest'.

ACTIVISM

I know in my heart that you do not wish to see the orang-utan become extinct, or the snowy owl. Do you? Sadly, many of the creatures featured in this book have already become extinct: the dodo, sea cow, black mamo, black-fronted parakeet, Falkland Islands wolf, hoopoe starling, the quagga. All gone!

> cuil chadáin na hAithne
> nár chualaís fúithi . . .?
> ní hann di níos mó

> *the Athens caddisfly*
> *have you not heard . . .?*
> *extinct!*

I wouldn't like to see the snowy owl becoming extinct, or the Inuit word for it, *ookpik*. Would you? Words, languages everywhere, can become extinct, just like animals. As far as I know, *mispoon* is the word for a male snowy owl in Cree and *newish* is the female. Great words! But they could disappear. Easily! We, humans, are guardians of language and guardians of biodiversity (and these important matters are linked.)

We managed to destroy or neglect our environment in the past; so, too, the treasure houses of languages were neglected or deliberately destroyed. We're doing something, at last, for the environment but the future of endangered languages is very uncertain.

What happens when you read and write haiku? Over time, you become more sensitive, more compassionate, more aware of all life forms on Earth. The world needs activists, to protect endangered species, endangered languages–peaceful, loving, intelligent, responsible activists. Why not become a haiku activist! Or a language activist!

Including Irish-language haiku in *Snowy Owl* and other haiku books for young readers might seem to be an unusual thing to do. It's a language unfamiliar to most people on the planet. But I wouldn't be much of a language activist if I excluded the medium of my choice from this book: Irish is the oldest literary language in Europe, after Greek and Latin. One first step in language activism is simply helping to make people aware of the rich tapestry of languages in this world. Good idea?

Why not make a decision, now, to learn another language? It will open up another world to you. Honestly! Which language to pick? Any language! Maybe a micro-language with fewer than a million speakers; or if your ancestors spoke a language other than the language you are speaking today, that would be an obvious choice. A very interesting choice. It might connect you to your ancestors in a very special way!

In 2023, the University of West Virginia decided to stop teaching foreign languages and spend more time on subjects such as forensics. Bad move! Fewer languages? That means fewer windows to the world. Some American universities offer courses in Native American languages. Stanford offers courses in Hawaiian, Cherokee, Navajo, Yup'ik, Lakota, and Nahuatl.

When the Hawaiian language became smothered by English, the ecological wisdom contained in the language began to wither. 2023 saw cataclysmic fires in Hawaii: non-native grasses dried out too quickly, the secret–and sacred–connection to the land was weakened as English, a non-native language, rose to dominance, bringing all of its cultural baggage with it.

Why go back and learn an ancestral language? Why does a long jumper go back? She can't spring forward from where she is. She is not a frog! That's why. She must go back and take a running jump. Going back is the way to the future. To relearn the language of your ancestors could bring you closer to them, closer to your history, your roots.

Language activism has been described as 'noble work' by Ben Okon, an activist for a Nigerian language known as Efik. A world language, such as English, facilitates communication but we should not drift, mindlessly, towards a monocultural, monolingual world. Such a trend would make soulless robots of us all, depriving us of the sounds and rhythms our ancestors shaped to sing a lullaby, whisper a prayer or love poem, utter a proverb, narrate a fable or myth, or explain the meaning and uses of a plant, or the story behind the name of a mountain or lake.

Jacey-Firth Hagen is an activist for a language which most of us probably never heard of: Gwich'in. She says,

> *Language activism is giving back to my family, peoples, and ancestors. For so long, our indigenous languages were silenced, due to assimilation policies used in attempts such as Indian (Indigenous) Residential Schools to destroy our identities as indigenous peoples. Our languages are a direct example of our identity, who we are, and where we come from–representing our ancestral relationship with the landscape and the abundance of plants and animals that have nurtured us since time immemorial.*

It makes sense, doesn't it? A haiku poet should explore our ancestral relationship with the landscape and the indigenous understanding of plants and animals. Indeed, I would love to see a flowering of haiku in the endangered languages of the world.

William Fanene is another language activist:

I am trying to facilitate social change through daily marketing campaigns aimed at preserving the Samoan language, particularly to those of Samoan heritage living outside of Samoa.

OOKPIK

Our cover artist for both *Orang-Utan* and *Snowy Owl*, Samuel Jessurun de Mesquita, was a Holocaust victim. Was de Mesquita aware of the significance of the *ookpik*–the snowy owl–in Inuit culture? One of the duties of the *ookpik* is to gather the souls of the dead and bring them safely to the spirit world before the break of day.

A photo of Samuel Jessurun de Mesquita, in happier times. Samuel's pet name was Sampie. This photo of a smiling Sampie was taken by his brother, Joseph.

Samuel's wife was also murdered by the Nazis, as was his son, Jaap. This is a portrait which his father made of Jaap in 1915:

Guide us, ookpik, guide us!

END

Further Reading:

ORANG-UTAN
Órang-Útan

Gabriel Rosenstock

"Gabriel Rosenstock is one of the most original, untypical and inventive writers/thinkers/poets in the world."
                                                           World Haiku Review

Gabriel Rosenstock in Paunar Ashram, Wardha, India, an ashram founded by Vinoba Bhave, a disciple of Gandhi, for the spiritual advancement of women. In Paunar, women dedicate their lives to rishi kheti, farming with simple tools, without the help of bullocks, and spinning cloth. The memoirs of Vinoba Bhave are called Moved by Love and in it he says, wisely: 'Without women, men alone cannot bring about world peace which is the crying need of our present times.' Amen.

Other Haiku & Senryu Titles of Interest

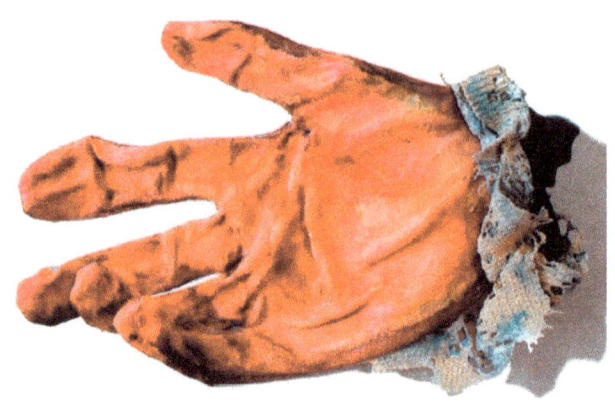

Give Me Your Hand
(ISBN: 9781068540837)
Haiku for children 8–13+ with an
international gallery of engaging artwork

"Creates an immersive experience that lingers long after reading."

Iliyana Stoyanova, Blithe Spirit,
Journal of the British Haiku Society, Vol. 35, No.3

LONELINESS
Uaigneas
Gabriel Rosenstock

Loneliness
(ISBN: 9781739561048)
Haiku for children 8–13+ with an
international gallery of superb artwork

"The haiku in this collection are contemplative, sometimes whimsical, and invite readers to find companionship in the smallest moments of existence."

Iliyana Stoyanova, Blithe Spirit,
Journal of the British Haiku Society, Vol. 35, No.3

Fluttering Their Way Into My Head
(ISBN: 9781782010883)
An exploration of haiku for young readers

Tea wi the Abbot
(ISBN: 9780993421754)
Bilingual selection of haiku by
John McDonald, in Scots and Irish

Snow / Sneachta: the snow haiku of Issa
(ISBN: 9780995622531)

A Sweater for the Tayfel
Bilingual haiku in response to
artwork by Issacher Ber Rybek
(Ukraine)
(Buttonhook Press, 2022)

Eye of the Fish
Bilingual haiku in response
to photographs by
Debiprasad Mukherjee
(Buttonhook Press, 2023)

Popocatépetl
(ISBN: 9780893044497)
Haiku for readers 8-12+ with an
international gallery of stupendous
artwork

www.ingramcontent.com/pod-product-compliance
Lightning Source LLC
Chambersburg PA
CBHW061232070526
44584CB00030B/4084